SECRETS OF
SELF-ACCEPTANCE

J. Donald Walters

Hardbound edition, second printing 1997

Copyright ©1993
J. Donald Walters

Illustrations copyright © 1995
Crystal Clarity, Publishers

Interior Illustrations: Sarah Moffat

ISBN 1-56589-043-4
10 9 8 7 6 5 4 3 2

Printed in China

Crystal ℞ Clarity
P U B L I S H E R S

14618 Tyler Foote Road, Nevada City, CA 95959
1-800-424-1055

exclude inconvenient realities from our lives, we'll find peace at last.

Unfortunately for those of us who succumb to this temptation, withdrawal and self-enclosure afford false security. Any attempt to banish the "barbarians" into outer darkness only makes our problems loom all the larger and more menacing, as we ourselves grow ever smaller. The more the ego withdraws into itself, the more painfully aware it becomes of its own limitations and inadequacy. The difficulty people have with accepting themselves as they are is rooted in their contractive consciousness, and not in any other flaws they may have. It isn't themselves they can't accept: It's their increasing sense of littleness. Littleness mocks the universal life-urge in all of us for self-expansion.

In the contractive mode, the very effort to accept oneself as he is only further affirms his littleness and pain. Any attempt, moreover, to objectify that pain by blaming it on others only causes further self-contraction, and an increase of pain.

The way back to self-acceptance, then, is not to begin with affirmations of self-worth. Such affirmations can only force comparison with other people: "I'm just as worthy as he is"; "I'm *more* worthy than he is!"; "he's preventing me from developing a sense of my own worthiness!" Statements like these are typical reflections of a contractive mind. The cure lies in self-forgetfulness, not in self-affirmation.

The way back to self-acceptance is, first, to get into an expansive mode by affirming a more generous, giving attitude toward others. Only after cultivating an expansive outlook can a person see himself accurately in his relation to others, and to the greater scheme of things.

Later, from an expanded perspective, it will be possible for him to affirm his independence of other people, or non-dependence on them, without at the same time affirming those attitudes of self-withdrawal which make a person forever—in his own mind at least—a victim of life. At this point, one can affirm safely at last his own integrity in relation to others, and to Life as a whole.

While traveling the road back to self-acceptance, bear in mind that you, in common with every other human being, are unique. The melody you have to sing is yours alone for all eternity. The role you have to play on Life's stage can be played by no one else. Your allotted task is to learn to play it to perfection. That melody, however, or that role, belongs to a more expanded selfhood than the realities you experience in your little ego. Transcend all limitation by contemplating ever-more-expanding vistas of reality. Ultimately, you will discover who you *really* are, behind all the ego masks that you—in common with most human beings—wear.

The "secrets" contained in this little book follow a definite sequence: from the ego-squeeze of self-rejection to the relaxation and joy that accompany self-expansion and total self-acceptance.

DAY ONE

The secret of self-acceptance is...

realizing your uniqueness in the entire universe. No one will ever have your song to sing: Through all eternity it will be yours alone. Your primary task in life is to learn to sing that song to perfection.

DAY TWO

The secret of self-acceptance is...

accepting others, first, as *they* are.
Only then will you be able
to accept yourself as *you* are.

DAY THREE

The secret of self-acceptance is...

not envying others their talents and accomplishments. It is better even to fail in one's own soul-appointed duty than to succeed in someone else's. Once you succeed in being wholly yourself, you will have achieved the most glorious success possible for any human being.

DAY FOUR

The secret of self-acceptance is...

not resenting anyone;
for by resentment
we only belittle ourselves.

DAY FIVE

The secret of self-acceptance is...

respecting everyone; for as we are,
so do we imagine others to be;
and as we view them,
so do we ourselves become even more.

DAY SIX

The secret of self-acceptance is...

mixing with those who, in their own expansiveness, offer support to others. Shun the company of those who are cynical or insecure.

DAY SEVEN

The secret of self-acceptance is...

loving others,
and not waiting for them
first to love you.

DAY EIGHT

The secret of self-acceptance is...

serving others
ever more consciously
as an instrument
of a Higher Power.

DAY NINE

The secret of self-acceptance is...

forgiving others; for as we forgive,
so are we ourselves forgiven by them,
and by Life itself.
By forgiving others, we acquire also
the wisdom to forgive *ourselves*.

DAY TEN

The secret of self-acceptance is...

not expecting too much of others,
for only thereby do we learn
not to expect too much of ourselves.

DAY ELEVEN

The secret of self-acceptance is...

not blaming others for their negative
attitudes and behavior toward us;
for in blaming them
we only weaken ourselves,
and give them power to hurt us.

DAY TWELVE

The secret of self-acceptance is...

not blaming yourself.
Always remember,
the more important the painting,
the longer the time
and the greater the effort required
to carry it through to perfection.

DAY THIRTEEN

The secret of self-acceptance is...

uprooting negative expectations
from the mind, and sowing
positive ones instead.
For like attracts like.
A person's destiny is molded
to a great extent by the expectations
he holds of life.

DAY FOURTEEN

The secret of self-acceptance is...

not giving yourself too much importance,
nor taking yourself too seriously.
Your true importance
will increase proportionately
to how little of it you claim for yourself.

DAY FIFTEEN

The secret of self-acceptance is...

expanding your sense of selfhood,
and including others in your greater self.
View their happiness, their fulfillment,
their successes as your own.

DAY SIXTEEN

The secret of self-acceptance is...

not taking your mistakes too seriously.
Calmly determine that you'll simply
do better next time.

DAY SEVENTEEN

The secret of self-acceptance is...

not identifying yourself
with your mistakes. They are not yours,
but were simply there to be made
by anyone who is striving sincerely
toward perfection.

DAY EIGHTEEN

The secret of self-acceptance is...

not identifying yourself with failure.
Neither success nor failure
can define you, who are made
in the image of Infinite Perfection.

DAY NINETEEN

The secret of self-acceptance is...

to raise your level of energy
by developing an attitude of willingness.
Do willingly and cheerfully
whatever needs to be done.

DAY TWENTY

The secret of self-acceptance is...

getting sufficient exercise; breathing
deeply; sitting and standing erect;
eating properly. Eat a preponderance
of fruits and vegetables, and less meat.
A healthy body makes for
healthy attitudes in life.

DAY TWENTY-ONE

The secret of self-acceptance is...

a sense of humor;
above all, learning to laugh at yourself.
It will give you a right sense of
proportion. Read one funny story a day.
Share at least one good joke every day
with your friends.

DAY TWENTY-TWO

The secret of self-acceptance is...

taking responsibility
for whatever happens to you.
For nothing occurs without a cause,
a cause which, usually,
can be traced to some attitude,
some expectation—perhaps held only
subconsciously—in yourself.

DAY TWENTY-THREE

The secret of self-acceptance is...

not allowing the weeds of guilt
to grow in the garden of your faith in
yourself that you are trying to cultivate.
Reflect, all human beings are prone to
error. Transform feelings of guilt
into a resolution to do ever better.

DAY TWENTY-FOUR

The secret of self-acceptance is...

to laugh with others,
if they tease you.
Don't take their words
too deeply to heart.

DAY TWENTY-FIVE

The secret of self-acceptance is...

a positive attitude.
A wise man once said,
"Conditions are essentially neutral.
Your attitude will determine whether
they seem, to you, positive or negative."

DAY TWENTY-SIX

The secret of self-acceptance is...

not trying to justify yourself
in others' eyes. Be complete in yourself.
Do your best by your own understanding,
then accept the consequences
with equanimity. Bear in mind that the
highest Judge of your behavior
resides forever within you.

DAY TWENTY-SEVEN

The secret of self-acceptance is...

not conditioning your happiness,
nor the truths you hold dear,
by the opinions of others.

DAY TWENTY-EIGHT

The secret of self-acceptance is...

being centered in your own inner reality,
and not allowing yourself to be victimized
by others' definitions of right or wrong.

DAY TWENTY-NINE

The secret of self-acceptance is...

being concerned with pleasing God, and
your own higher conscience—not other
people, except as they may help to clarify
or confirm for you the Higher Will.

DAY THIRTY

The secret of self-acceptance is...

being grateful for
whatever tests you attract in life,
for they are means
by which you can grow
in strength and wisdom.

DAY THIRTY-ONE

The secret of self-acceptance is...

concentrating on
your potential for self-improvement.
Love that potential,
not your present state of imperfection.
Affirm that what is yours *potentially*
is forever yours already.

OTHER BOOKS
IN THE SECRETS SERIES
by J. Donald Walters

Secrets of Love
Secrets of Friendship
Secrets of Happiness
Secrets for Men
Secrets for Women
Secrets of Marriage
Secrets of Success
Secrets of Prosperity
Secrets of Leadership

Secrets of Winning People
Secrets of Meditation
Secrets of Inner Peace
Secrets of Emotional Healing
Secrets of Radiant Health and Well-Being

(*for children*)
Life's Little Secrets
Little Secrets of Success
Little Secrets of Happiness
Little Secrets of Friendship

SELECTED OTHER TITLES
by J. Donald Walters

Expansive Marriage

Money Magnetism

Education for Life

The Artist as a Channel

The Art of Supportive Leadership

Affirmations for Self-Healing

The Path (*the autobiography of* J. Donald Walters)

*For information about these or other Crystal Clarity
books, tapes, or products call:*
1-800-424-1055

Secrets of Winning People
Secrets of Meditation
Secrets of Inner Peace
Secrets of Emotional Healing
Secrets of Radiant Health and Well-Being

(*for children*)
Life's Little Secrets
Little Secrets of Success
Little Secrets of Happiness
Little Secrets of Friendship

SELECTED OTHER TITLES
by J. Donald Walters

Expansive Marriage

Money Magnetism

Education for Life

The Artist as a Channel

The Art of Supportive Leadership

Affirmations for Self-Healing

The Path (*the autobiography of* J. Donald Walters)

*For information about these or other Crystal Clarity
books, tapes, or products call:*
1-800-424-1055